To

_____

From

_____

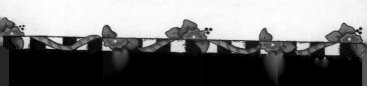

You Are Special

Scripture quotations are from the following sources: The Holy Bible,
New International Version® (NIV), © 1973, 1978, 1984 by
International Bible Society. Used by permission of Zondervan
Publishing House. The Holy Bible, New Century Version (NCV),
© 1987, 1988, 1991 by Word Publishing, Dallas, Texas 75039. Used
by permission. The Message (MSG), © 1993, 1994, 1995, 1996.
Used by permission of NavPress Publishing Group. The Living Bible
(TLB) © 1971. Used by permission of Tyndale House Publishers,
Inc., Wheaton, Illinois 60189. All rights reserved.

ISBN 1-58061-357-8

January 1

Life begins each morning.... Each morning is the open door to a new world—new vistas, new aims, new tryings.

Leigh Hodges

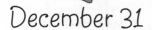

December 31

A new year can begin only because
the old year ends.
Madeleine L'Engle

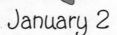

January 2

Every day under the sun is a gift. Receive it with eagerness. Treat it kindly. Share it with joy. Each night return it to the Giver who will make it bright and shiny again before the next sunrise.

December 30

God takes care of all who stay close to him.
Psalm 31:23 MSG

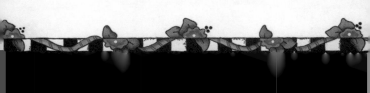

January 3

Friendship is one of the sweetest joys of life.
Charles H. Spurgeon

December 29

May you always find three welcomes in life,
In a garden during summer,
At a fireside during winter,
And whatever the day or season
In the kind eyes of a friend.

January 4

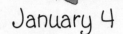

There is always a time for gratitude
and new beginnings.
J. Robert Moskin

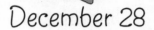

December 28

Dear friends, no matter how we find them, are as essential to our lives as breathing in and breathing out.

Lois Wyse

January 5

Be truly glad! There is wonderful joy ahead.

1 Peter 1:6 TLB

December 27

Still round the corner there may wait,
A new road, or a secret gate.
J. R. R. Tolkien

January 6

Live as though you believe that the power behind the
universe is a power of love, a personal power of love,
a love so great that all of us really do matter to Him.

Madeleine L'Engle

December 26

Many merry Christmases, many happy New Years.
Unbroken friendships, great accumulations
of cheerful recollections and affections on earth,
and heaven for us all.

Charles Dickens

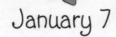

January 7

Just the knowledge that a good book is awaiting one
at the end of a long day makes that day happier.

Kathleen Norris

December 25

For to us a child is born, to us a son is given, and the government will be on his shoulders. And he will be called Wonderful Counselor, Mighty God, Everlasting Father, Prince of Peace.

Isaiah 9:6 NIV

January 8

A friend listens to your words but hears your heart.

December 24

God grant you the light in Christmas, which is faith;
the warmth of Christmas, which is love...
the all of Christmas, which is Christ.

Wilda English

January 9

Living is the constant adjustment of thought to life and life to thought in such a way that we are always growing, always experiencing new things in the old and old things in the new.

Thomas Merton

December 23

The heart of the giver makes the gift dear and precious.

Martin Luther

January 10

Take delight in the Lord, and he will give you
the desires of your heart.
Psalm 37:4 NRSV

December 22

For somehow, not only at Christmas, but all the long
year through, the joy that you give to others
is the joy that comes back to you.
John Greenleaf Whittier

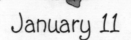

January 11

A friend is able to see you as the wonderful
person God created you to be.
Ann D. Parrish

December 21

Every time you smile at someone, it is an action of love, a gift to that person, a beautiful thing.
Mother Teresa

January 12

Life is so full of meaning and purpose, so full of
beauty—beneath its covering—that you will find
that earth but cloaks your heaven.

Fra Giovanni

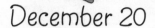

December 20

"The virgin will be with child and give birth to
a son, and they will call Him Immanuel"—
which means, "God with us."
Matthew 1:23 NIV

January 13

What we do does not give us simplicity, but it does put us in the place where we can receive it. It sets our lives before God in such a way that He can work into us the grace of simplicity.

Richard J. Foster

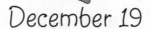

December 19

When we recall the past, we usually find that it is the simplest things—not the great occasions—that in retrospect give off the greatest glow of happiness.

Bob Hope

January 14

A friend is the hope of the heart.
Ralph Waldo Emerson

December 18

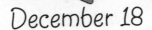

God's peace is joy resting.
His joy is peace dancing.
F. F. Bruce

January 15

Look to the Lord and his strength; seek his face always.
Remember the wonders he has done.
Psalm 105:4-5 NIV

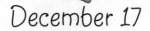

December 17

Christmas is when God came down the stairs of heaven with a baby in His arms.

January 16

True contentment is a real, even an active, virtue—not only affirmative but creative. It is the power of getting out of any situation all there is in it.

G. K. Chesterton

December 16

Happiness is being at peace, being with loved ones,
being comfortable. But most of all,
it's having those loved ones.
Johnny Cash

January 17

I see in the stars, in the rivers, I see in the open fields,
patches of heaven and threads of paradise. Let me
sew the earth, the day, the way of my life into a
pattern that forms a quilt, God's quilt, to keep
me warm today and always.

Christopher de Vinck

December 15

May the Lord of peace himself give you
peace at all times and in every way.

2 Thessalonians 3:16 NIV

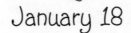

January 18

There are no little things. "Little things," so called,
are the hinges of the universe.

Fanny Fern

December 14

Our road will be smooth and untroubled
no matter what care life may send;
If we travel the pathway together,
and walk side by side with a friend.
Henry Van Dyke

January 19

A joyful heart is like the sunshine of God's love,
the hope of eternal happiness.

Mother Teresa

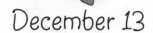

December 13

God gave me friends so I wouldn't have to laugh alone.

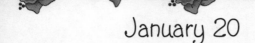

January 20

Do to others as you would have them do to you.

Luke 6:31 NRSV

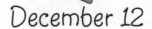

December 12

The things that matter the most in this world,
they can never be held in our hand.
Gloria Gaither

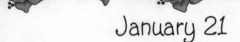

January 21

There are times when encouragement means such a lot.
And a word is enough to convey it.
Grace Stricker Dawson

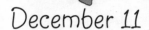

December 11

A friend is a gift you give yourself.
Robert Louis Stevenson

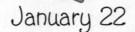

January 22

Blessed are the ones God sends to show
His love for us...our friends.

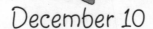

December 10

It is good and pleasant when God's
people live together in peace!
Psalm 133:1 NCV

January 23

If peace be in the heart the wildest winter
storm is full of solemn beauty.
C. F. Richardson

December 9

A friend is someone who understands your past,
believes in your future, and accepts you
today just the way you are.
Beverly LaHaye

January 24

The fountain of beauty is the heart, and every generous
thought illustrates the walls of your chamber.
Francis Quarles

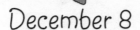

December 8

I believe that we are always attracted to what we need
most, an instinct leading us toward the persons
who are to open new vistas in our lives and
fill them with new knowledge.

Helene Iswolski

January 25

May the Lord continually bless you with heaven's blessings as well as with human joys.

Psalm 128:5 TLB

December 7

How many, many friendships
Life's path has let me see;
I've kept a scrap of each of them
To make the whole of me.

June Masters Bacher

January 26

A friend is what the heart needs all the time.
Henry Van Dyke

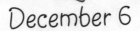

December 6

Clothe yourselves with compassion, kindness, humility, gentleness and patience.

Colossians 3:12 NIV

January 27

The realities of faith, hope, and love can make
every day an exciting adventure.
Norman Vincent Peale

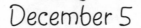

December 5

Happiness is intrinsic, it's an internal thing.
When you build it into yourself, no external
circumstances can take it away.
Leo Buscaglia

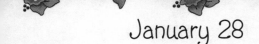

January 28

God is all that is good, as I see it—and the
goodness that all things have, it is He.
Julian of Norwich

December 4

Blessed are those who can give wtihout remembering,
and take without forgetting.
Elizabeth Bibesco

January 29

Celebration is more than a happy feeling.
Celebration is an experience. It is liking others,
accepting others, laughing with others.
Douglas R. Stuva

December 3

The heart generous and kind most resembles God.
Robert Burns

January 30

There is a friend who sticks closer than a brother.

Proverbs 18:24 TLB

December 2

Let me, if I may, be ever welcomed
to my room in winter by a glowing hearth,
in summer by a vase of flowers; if I may not,
let me think how nice they would be,
and bury myself in my work....
Let us acknowledge all good, all delight
that the world holds, and be content.

George MacDonald

January 31

God has a wonderful plan for each person.... He knew
even before He created this world what beauty He
would bring forth from our lives.

Louis B. Wyly

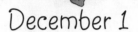

December 1

In quietness and in trust is your strength.
Isaiah 30:15 NIV

February 1

There is no joy in life like the joy of sharing.
Billy Graham

November 30

There is something very powerful about...someone
believing in you, someone giving you another chance.
Sheila Walsh

February 2

There is an exquisite melody in every heart. If we
listen closely, we can hear each other's song.
A friend knows the song in your heart and
responds with beautiful harmony.

November 29

Time is a very precious gift of God; so precious that it's only given to us moment by moment.

Amelia Barr

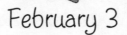

February 3

Our brightest blazes of gladness are commonly
kindled by unexpected sparks.
Samuel Johnson

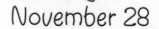

November 28

Friends...they cherish each other's hopes. They are kind to each other's dreams.

Henry David Thoreau

February 4

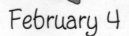

He surrounds me with lovingkindness and tender
mercies. He fills my life with good things!
Psalm 103:4-5 TLB

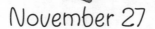

November 27

Trust your friends with both the delightful
and the difficult parts of your life.
Luci Shaw

February 5

I breathed a song into the air;
It fell to earth, I know not where.....
and the song, from beginning to end,
I found again in the heart of a friend.

Longfellow

November 26

Thanksgiving is a time of quiet reflection...an annual
reminder that God has, again, been ever so faithful.
The solid and simple things of life are
brought into clear focus.

Charles Swindoll

February 6

The most universally awesome experience that mankind knows is to stand alone on a clear night and look at the stars. It was God who first set the stars in space; He is their Maker and Master.... Such are His power and His majesty.

J. I. Packer

November 25

Give thanks to the Lord, for he is good;
his love endures forever.

Psalm 106:1 NIV

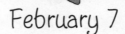

February 7

Every morning is a fresh opportunity to find God's
extraordinary joy in the most ordinary places.

Janet Weaver Smith

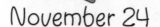

November 24

True gratitude, like true love, must find
expression in acts, not words.

R. Mildred Barker

February 8

I have learned that to have a good friend is the
purest of all God's gifts, for it is a love that
has no exchange of payment.

Frances Farmer

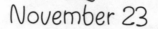

November 23

There is something in every season, in every day,
to celebrate with thanksgiving.
Gloria Gaither

February 9

God has given each of you some special abilities;
be sure to use them to help each other, passing on
to others God's many kinds of blessings.

1 Peter 4:10 TLB

November 22

Cherish your human connections: your relationships with friends and family.

Barbara Bush

February 10

It doesn't take monumental feats to make the world
a better place. It can be as simple as letting someone
go ahead of you in a grocery line.
Barbara Johnson

November 21

There is always something for which to be thankful.
Charles Dickens

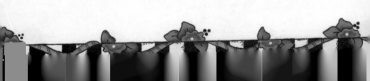

February 11

My fondest hope is that I may be worthy
of a place in your friendship, and being admitted
to that sacred circle, that I may never prove
unfaithful to your trust in me.

Edwin Osgood Grover

November 20

Give thanks in all circumstances.
1 Thessalonians 5:18 NIV

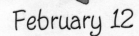

February 12

Friends find the sweetest sense of happiness comes
from simply being together.

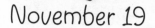

November 19

To know someone here or there with whom you feel
there is an understanding in spite of distances
or thoughts unexpressed—that can make
of this earth a garden.

Goethe

February 13

A true friend inspires you to believe the best in yourself, to keep pursuing your deepest dreams. Most wonderful of all, she celebrates all your successes as if they were her own!

November 18

If you surrender completely to the moments as they pass, you live more richly those moments.
Anne Morrow Lindbergh

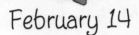

February 14

Whatever you do, do it with kindness and love.
1 Corinthians 16:14 TLB

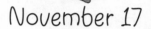

November 17

There can be no intimacy without conversation.
To know and love a friend over the years
you must have regular talks.
Alan Loy McGinnis

February 15

No love, no friendship can cross the path of our destiny
without leaving some mark on it forever.

François Mauriac

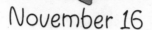

November 16

Friendship: It involves many things, but above all, the power of going out of one's self and seeing and appreciating whatever is noble and loving in another.

Thomas Hughes

February 16

Simplicity means a return to the posture of
dependence. Like children we live in a spirit of trust.
What we have we receive as a gift.
Richard J. Foster

November 15

I have not stopped giving thanks for you,
remembering you in my prayers.
Ephesians 1:16 NIV

February 17

What brings joy to the heart is not so much the friend's gifts as the friend's love.

Aelred of Rievaulx

November 14

Thank you, Lord, for the grace of your love,
for the grace of friendship,
and for the grace of beauty.

Henri J. M. Nouwen

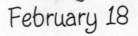

February 18

It isn't the big pleasures that count the most;
it's making a great deal out of the little ones.
Jean Webster

November 13

God created us with an overwhelming desire to soar....
He designed us to be tremendously productive and "to
mount up with wings like eagles," realistically dreaming
of what He can do with our potential.

Carol Kent

February 19

The Lord is good to all, and his compassion
is over all that he has made.

Psalm 145:9 NRSV

November 12

A good friend will sharpen your character,
draw your soul into the light, and challenge
your heart to love in a greater way.

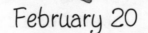

February 20

A true friend is one who is concerned about what we are becoming, who sees beyond the present relationship, and who cares deeply about us as a whole person.

Gloria Gaither

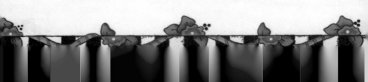

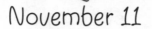

November 11

Promises may get friends, but it's
performances that keep them.

Owen Feltham

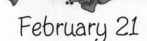

February 21

Your greatest pleasure is that which rebounds from
hearts that you have made glad.
Henry Ward Beecher

November 10

Oh, give thanks to the Lord, for he is so good!
For his lovingkindness is forever.
Psalm 118:29 TLB

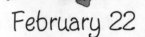

February 22

Simplicity is completely absorbed in
listening to what it hears.
Thomas Merton

November 9

One of the highest compliments I can receive
is that I am your friend.

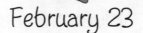

February 23

Looking forward to things is half
the pleasure of them.

Lucy Maud Montgomery

November 8

Into all our lives, in many simple, familiar, homely ways, God infuses this element of joy from the surprises of life, which unexpectedly brighten our days, and fill our eyes with light.

Longfellow

February 24

Great is your love, reaching to the heavens;
your faithfulness reaches to the skies.

Psalm 57:10 NIV

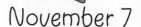

November 7

The beauty of the earth, the beauty of the sky, the order of the stars, the sun, the moon...their very loveliness is their confession of God.

Augustine

February 25

A pleasant companion reduces the length of a journey.
Syrus

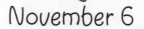

November 6

Friends remind us we are part of something
greater than ourselves, a larger world.
Barbara Jenkins

February 26

If we celebrate the years behind us
they become stepping-stones of strength
and joy for the years ahead.

November 5

Dear friend, I pray that you may enjoy good health
and that all may go well with you.

3 John 1:2 NIV

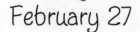

February 27

A friend is a person with whom
I may be sincere, before whom
I may think out loud.
Ralph Waldo Emerson

November 4

It is an extraordinary and beautiful thing that God, in creation...works with the beauty of matter; the reality of things; the discoveries of the senses, all five of them; so that we, in turn, may hear the grass growing; see a face springing to life in love and laughter.... The offerings of creation...our glimpses of truth.

Madeleine L'Engle

February 28

Much of what is sacred is hidden in the ordinary,
everyday moments of our lives. To see something of
the sacred in those moments takes slowing down so we
can live our lives more reflectively.

Ken Gire

November 3

We must know that we have been created for greater things, not just to be a number in the world.... We have been created in order to love and to be loved.

Mother Teresa

February 29

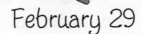

May you be given more and more of God's
kindness, peace, and love.

Jude 1:2 TLB

November 2

Whole hearted, ready laughter heals, encourages, relaxes anyone within hearing distance. The laughter that springs from love makes wide the space around— gives room for the loved one to enter in.

Eugenia Price

March 1

A friend is somebody who loves us with
understanding, as well as emotion.
Robert Louis Stevenson

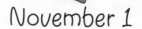

November 1

I especially value the friends who love me as God
loves me—through no merit of my own!
Sharon M. Mason

March 2

Let us believe that God is in all our simple deeds
and learn to find Him there.
A. W. Tozer

October 31

A generous person will be enriched, and one
who gives water will get water.
Proverbs 11:25 NRSV

March 3

Friends...lift our spirits, keep us honest, stick with us when times are tough, and make mundane tasks enjoyable. No wonder we want to make friends.

Em Griffin

October 30

A friend is one who says, I've time,
When others have to rush.
June Masters Bacher

March 4

May your footsteps set you upon a lifetime journey of love. May you wake each day with His blessings and sleep each night in His keeping. And may you always walk in His tender care.

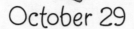

October 29

To live is so startling it leaves little
time for anything else.
Emily Dickinson

March 5

Love...binds everything together in perfect harmony.
Colossians 3:14 NRSV

October 28

Purity and simplicity
Are the two wings
with which we soar
above the earth
And all temporary nature...
Simplicity turns to God;
purity unites with and enjoys Him.

Thomas à Kempis

March 6

Sometimes it is a slender thread,
Sometimes a strong, stout rope;
She clings to one end,
I the other;
She calls it friendship;
I call it hope.

Lois Wyse

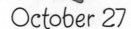

October 27

The best and most beautiful things in the
world cannot be seen or even touched.
They must be felt with the heart.
Helen Keller

March 7

That is God's call to us—simply to be people who are
content to live close to Him and to renew the kind of
life in which the closeness is felt and experienced.

Thomas Merton

October 26

May the Lord be loyal to you...and reward you with
many demonstrations of his love!

2 Samuel 2:6 TLB

March 8

The glory of friendship is found in the inspiration that comes when I discover that someone else believes in me and is willing to trust me with their friendship.

October 25

Wishing to be friends is quick work,
but friendship is a slow ripening fruit.
Aristotle

March 9

We all stumble, every one of us. That's why it's a comfort to go hand in hand.

Emily Kimbrough

October 24

Perfection consists simply in...being just
what God wants us to be.

Thérèse of Lisieux

March 10

Carry each other's burdens.
Galatians 6:2 NIV

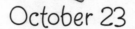

October 23

Happiness is excitement that has found a settling down place, but there is always a little corner that keeps flapping around.

E. L. Konigsburg

March 11

You are God's created beauty and the focus
of His affection and delight.
Janet Weaver Smith

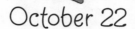

October 22

A friend is one who joyfully sings with you when you
are on the mountain top, and silently walks
beside you through the valley.
William A. Ward

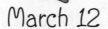

March 12

There is no duty we so much underrate as the duty of being happy. By being happy we sow anonymous benefits upon the world.

Robert Louis Stevenson

October 21

You're my place of quiet retreat; I wait for your
Word to renew me.... Therefore I lovingly
embrace everything you say.

Psalm 119:114,119 MSG

March 13

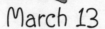

Friendship is the breathing rose,
with sweets in every fold.
Oliver Wendell Holmes

October 20

All that is worth cherishing begins in the heart.
Suzanne Chapin

March 14

Eating lunch with a friend. Trying to do a decent day's work. Hearing the rain patter against the window. There is no event so commonplace but that God is present within it, always hiddenly, always leaving you room to recognize Him or not to recognize Him.

Frederich Buechner

October 19

The best things are nearest: breath in your nostrils, light in your eyes, flowers at your feet, duties at your hand, the path of God just before you.

Robert Louis Stevenson

March 15

When we obey him, every path he guides us on is fragrant with his lovingkindness and his truth.
Psalm 25:10 TLB

October 18

Better without gold than without a friend.

March 16

Life begets life. Energy creates energy. It is by
spending oneself that one becomes rich.
Sarah Bernhardt

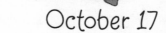

October 17

God bless the friend who sees my needs
and reaches out a hand,
who lifts me up, who prays for me,
and helps me understand.

Amanda Bradley

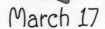

March 17

Everything in life is most fundamentally a gift.
And you receive it best, and you live it best,
by holding it with very open hands.
Leo O'Donovan

October 16

Love is patient, love is kind.... It always protects,
always trusts, always hopes, always perseveres.
Love never fails.
1 Corinthians 13:4,7-8 NIV

March 18

Friendships multiply joys and divide griefs.
Henry George Bohn

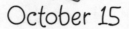

October 15

It is a gift of God to us to be able
to share our love with others.

Mother Teresa

March 19

Right now a moment of time is fleeting by!
Capture its reality.... Become that moment.
Paul Cezanne

October 14

Far away, there in the sunshine, are my highest
aspirations.... I can look up and see their beauty, believe
in them, and try to follow where they lead.
Louisa May Alcott

March 20

When we love each other God lives in us and his
love within us grows ever stronger.

1 John 4:12 TLB

October 13

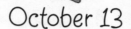

A friend by your side can keep you warmer
than the most expensive coat.

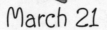

March 21

You're my friend—
What a thing friendship is, world without end!
Robert Browning

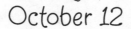

October 12

I am beginning to learn that it is the sweet, simple things of life which are the real ones after all.

Laura Ingalls Wilder

March 22

I will always keep the memories
of the special joys we have
shared close to my heart.

October 11

Dear friends, let us practice loving each other, for love comes from God and those who are loving and kind show that they are the children of God.

1 John 4:7 TLB

March 23

If instead of a gem, or even a flower, we should cast
the gift of a loving thought into the heart of a friend;
that would be giving as the angels give.
George MacDonald

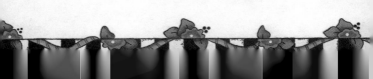

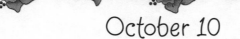

October 10

Love is the seed of all hope. It is the enticement
to trust, to risk, to try, to go on.
Gloria Gaither

March 24

The real key to friendship
Is a tender, gentle blend
Of this plain and simple truth—
That one must be a friend.

Edith H. Shank

October 9

Getting things accomplished isn't nearly
as important as taking time for love.
Janette Oke

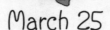

March 25

If I rise on the wings of the dawn, if I settle on the far
side of the sea, even there your hand will guide me,
your right hand will hold me fast.

Psalm 139:9-10 NIV

October 8

The best friendships have weathered misunderstandings and trying times. One of the secrets of a good relationship is the ability to accept the storms.
Alan Loy McGinnis

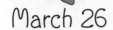

March 26

Just to be is a blessing. Just to live is holy.
Abraham Joshua Heschel

October 7

Joy is warm and radiant and clamors
for expressions and experience.
Dorothy Segovia

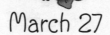

March 27

Joy is the echo of God's life within us.
Joseph Marmion

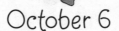

October 6

Live in harmony and peace. And may the
God of love and peace be with you.
2 Corinthians 13:11 TLB

March 28

Open your hearts to the love God instills....
God loves you tenderly. What He gives you is not
to be kept under lock and key, but to be shared.

Mother Teresa

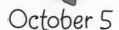

October 5

Of all best things upon the earth,
I hold that a faithful friend is the best.
Edward Bulwer-Lytton

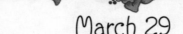

March 29

Friends are an indispensable part of a meaningful life.
They are the ones who share our burdens
and multiply our blessings.
Beverly LaHaye

October 4

Keep your face to the sunshine and you
cannot see the shadows.
Helen Keller

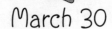

March 30

Whatever is true, whatever is noble, whatever is right,
whatever is pure, whatever is lovely, whatever
is admirable—if anything is excellent or praiseworthy—
think about such things.

Philippians 4:8 NIV

October 3

Take a risk. Open up your heart. Find a real friend and grow together. Be a real friend and see what happens.

Sheila Walsh

March 31

Friends find the sweetest sense of happiness comes
from simply being together.

October 2

That friendship only is indeed genuine when two friends, without speaking a word to each other, can nevertheless find happiness in being together.

George Ebers

April 1

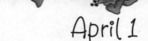

Recall it as often as you wish, a happy
memory never wears out.
Libbie Fudim

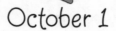

October 1

The steadfast love of the Lord is from everlasting to everlasting on those who fear him, and his righteousness to children's children.

Psalm 103:17 NRSV

April 2

A good friend is a connection to life—a tie to the past, a road to the future, the key to sanity in a totally insane world.

Lois Wyse

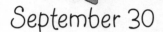

September 30

Friendship is the fruit gathered from the trees planted
in the rich soil of love, and nurtured with
tender care and understanding.

Alma L. Weixelbaum

April 3

If we just give God the little that we have,
we can trust Him to make it go around.

Gloria Gaither

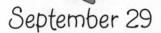

September 29

Kind words are jewels that live in the heart and soul
and remain as blessed memories years
after they have been spoken.

Marvea Johnson

April 4

Love...always protects, always trusts,
always hopes, always perseveres.
1 Corinthians 13:6,7 NIV

September 28

What is important is that one is capable of love. It is perhaps the only glimpse we are permitted of eternity.

Helen Hayes

April 5

Jesus cannot forget us; we have been graven
on the palms of His hands.

Lois Picillo

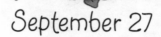

September 27

The fabric of life would be unadorned without the ribbons and lace added by friendship.

April 6

I count your friendship one of the chiefest pleasures
of my life, a comfort in time of doubt and trouble,
a joy in time of prosperity and success,
and an inspiration at all times.

Edwin Osgood Grover

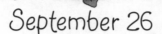

September 26

May the Lord keep watch between you and me
when we are away from each other.

Genesis 31:49 NIV

April 7

All the things in this world are gifts and signs of God's love to us. The whole world is a love letter from God.

Peter Kreeft

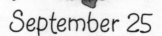

September 25

Friendship cheers like a sunbeam; charms like a good story; inspires like a brave leader; binds like a golden chain; guides like a heavenly vision.

Newell Dwight Hillis

April 8

Blue skies with white clouds on summer days.
A myriad of stars on clear moonlit nights. Tulips
and roses and violets and dandelions and daisies.
Bluebirds and laughter and sunshine and Easter.
See how He loves us!

Alice Chapin

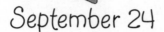

September 24

Where the soul is full of peace and joy, outward
surroundings and circumstances are
of comparatively little account.

Hannah Whitall Smith

April 9

Be...full of sympathy toward each other, loving one another with tender hearts and humble minds.

1 Peter 3:8 TLB

September 23

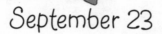

What we have once enjoyed we can never lose.
All that we love deeply becomes a part of us.

Helen Keller

April 10

You have a unique message to deliver, a unique song to sing, a unique act of love to bestow. This message, this song, and this act of love have been entrusted exclusively to the one and only you.

John Powell, S. J.

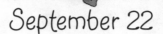

September 22

If we give God the little that we have, we can
trust Him to make it go around.
Gloria Gaither

April 11

The joyful birds prolong the strain,
their song with every spring renewed;
the air we breathe, and falling rain,
each softly whispers: God is good.

John Hampden Gurney

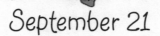

September 21

Perfume and incense bring joy to the heart, and
the pleasantness of one's friend springs
from his earnest counsel.

Proverbs 27:9 NIV

April 12

A loyal friend is like a safe shelter; find one,
and you have found a treasure.

Sirach

September 20

Silences make the real conversations between friends.
Not the saying but the never needing
to say is what counts.

Margaret Lee Runbeck

April 13

Were there no God we would be in this glorious world
with grateful hearts and no one to thank.
Christina Rossetti

September 19

We can do no great things, only small
things with great love.
Mother Teresa

April 14

Say only what is good and helpful to those you are talking to, and what will give them a blessing.

Ephesians 4:29 TLB

September 18

Life is fortified by many friendships. To love, and to be loved, is the greatest happiness of existence.

Sydney Smith

April 15

Don't ever let yourself get so busy that you miss those little but important extras in life—the beauty of a day, the smile of a friend, the serenity of a quiet moment alone. For it is often life's smallest pleasures and gentlest joys that make the biggest and most lasting difference.

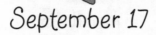

September 17

All we have and are is a gift of grace to be shared.
Lloyd John Ogilvie

April 16

Life is not intended to be simply a round of work,
no matter how interesting and important that work may
be. A moment's pause to watch the glory of a sunrise
or a sunset is soul satisfying, while a bird's song
will set the steps to music all day long.

Laura Ingalls Wilder

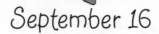

September 16

How kind he is! How good he is! So merciful, this God
of ours! The Lord protects the simple and the childlike.
Psalm 116:5-6 TLB

April 17

Good friends are like stars.... You don't always see them, but you know they are always there.

September 15

Joyfulness keeps the heart and face young.
A good laugh makes us better friends with
ourselves and everybody around us.

Orison Swett Marden

April 18

Never lose an opportunity of seeing anything that is
beautiful; for beauty is God's handwriting—
a wayside sacrament. Welcome it in every fair face,
in every fair sky, in every fair flower, and thank
God for it as a cup of blessing.

Ralph Waldo Emerson

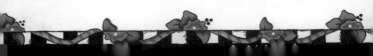

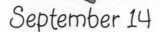

September 14

When we dream alone, it remains only a dream.
When we dream together, it is not just a dream.
It is the beginning of reality.
Dom Helder Camara

April 19

You give [us] drink from your river of delights. For with
you is the fountain of life; in your light we see light.
Psalm 36:8-9 NIV

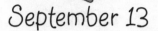

September 13

Friendship is like love at its best: not blind but sympathetically all-seeing; a support which does not wait for understanding; an act of faith which does not need, but always has, reason.

Louis Untermeyer

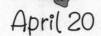

April 20

A friend is a gift whose worth cannot be
measured except by the heart.

September 12

Happy times and bygone days are never lost....
In truth, they grow more wonderful within
the heart that keeps them.

Kay Andrew

April 21

May God send His love like sunshine
in His warm and gentle way,
To fill each corner of your
heart each moment of today.

September 11

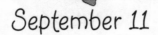

No one has greater love than this, to lay
down one's life for one's friends.

John 15:13 NRSV

April 22

Friendship...is the golden thread that ties
the hearts of all the world.
John Evelyn

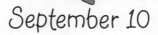

September 10

Little kindnesses, little acts of considerateness, little appreciations, little confidences...they are all that are needed to keep the friendship sweet.

Hugh Black

April 23

Allow your dreams a place in your prayers and plans.
God-given dreams can help you move into the
future He is preparing for you.

Barbara Johnson

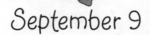

September 9

Every day in a life fills the whole life
with expectation and memory.
C. S. Lewis

April 24

The right word at the right time is like a custom-made
piece of jewelry, and a wise friend's timely reprimand
is like a gold ring slipped on your finger.

Proverbs 25:11-12 MSG

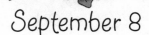

September 8

Grace and gratitude belong together like heaven and earth. Grace evokes gratitude like the voice an echo. Gratitude follows grace as thunder follows lightning.

Karl Barth

April 25

Sometimes our light goes out but is blown into flame by another human being. Each of us owes deepest thanks to those who have rekindled this light.

Albert Schweitzer

September 7

The day is done, the sun has set,
Yet light still tints the sky;
My heart stands still in reverence,
For God is passing by.

Ruth Alla Wager

April 26

To have a friend is to have one of the sweetest gifts
that life can bring; to be a friend is to have a solemn
and tender education of soul from day to day.

Amy Robertson Brown

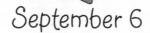

September 6

This is the day the Lord has made. We will
rejoice and be glad in it.
Psalm 118:24 TLB

April 27

The wonder of living is held within the beauty of silence, the glory of sunlight...the sweetness of fresh spring air, the quiet strength of earth, and the love that lies at the very root of all things.

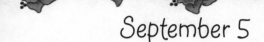

September 5

A friend is one who believes in you before
you believe in yourself.

April 28

The most beautiful discovery true friends make is that they can grow separately without growing apart.

Elisabeth Foley

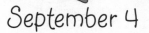

September 4

To be grateful is to recognize the love of God in everything He has given us—and He has given us everything. Every breath we draw is a gift of His love, every moment of existence a gift of grace.

Thomas Merton

April 29

We know that in all things God works for the good of those who love him.

Romans 8:28 NIV

September 3

Knowing what to say is not always necessary;
just the presence of a caring friend can make
a world of difference.

Sheri Curry

April 30

Friendship is a sheltering tree;
Oh, the joys that come down shower-like!
Samuel Taylor Coleridge

September 2

To speak gratitude is courteous and pleasant,
to enact gratitude is generous and noble, but to live
gratitude is to touch Heaven.

Johannes A. Gaertner

May 1

Love is the true means by which the world is enjoyed:
our love to others, and others' love to us.
Thomas Traherne

September 1

May the Lord bless and protect you; may the Lord's face radiate with joy because of you; may He be gracious to you, show you His favor, and give you His peace.

Numbers 6:24-26 TLB

May 2

All the flowers God has made are beautiful.
The rose in its glory and the lily in its whiteness
do not rob the tiny violet of its sweet smell,
or the daisy of its charming simplicity.

Thérèse of Lisieux

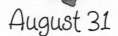

August 31

Laughing at ourselves as well as with each other gives a surprising sense of togetherness.

Hazel C. Lee

May 3

The steadfast love of the Lord never ceases, his
mercies never come to an end; they are new every
morning; great is your faithfulness.

Lamentations 3:22-23 NRSV

August 30

The good for which we are born into this world
is that we may learn to love.
George MacDonald

May 4

God moves in a mysterious way
His wonders to perform;
He plants His footsteps on the sea,
And rides upon the storm.

William Cowper

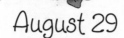

August 29

There is nothing on this earth more to be
prized than true friendship.

Thomas Aquinas

May 5

All the great blessings of my life are
present in my thoughts today.
Phoebe Cary

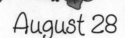

August 28

May the hand of a friend always be near you;
May God fill your heart with gladness to cheer you.

Irish Blessing

May 6

When you least expect it, a common thread—golden, at that—begins to weave together the fabric of friendship.
Mary Kay Shanley

August 27

I thank my God every time I remember you.

Philippians 1:3 NIV

May 7

Some people are so special that once they enter your life, it becomes richer and fuller and more wonderful than you ever thought it could be.

August 26

When our friends are present we ought to treat them
well; and when they are absent, to speak of them well.

Epictetus

May 8

The Lord who created you says...
"I have called you by name; you are mine."
Isaiah 43:1 TLB

August 25

We need both...the joy of the sense of sound;
and the equally great joy of its absence.

Madeleine L'Engle

May 10

In sunshine and in sorrow, we look for those
who will always stand with us.
Lois Wyse

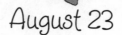

August 23

Few delights can equal the mere presence
of one whom we trust utterly.
George MacDonald

May 11

Friends help us feel secure. Our footing is surer when we know that someone accepts us as we are, someone has our best interests at heart, someone is always glad to see us, someone plans to stick around. There are few blessings like the blessing of a friend.

Emilie Barnes

August 22

A friend loves at all times.
Proverbs 17:17 NIV

May 12

When I look at the galaxies on a clear night—when I look at the incredible brilliance of creation, and think that this is what God is like, then instead of feeling intimidated and diminished by it, I am enlarged—I rejoice that I am part of it.

Madeleine L'Engle

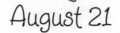

August 21

Do a deed of simple kindness;
Though its end you may not see,
It may reach, like widening ripples,
Down a long eternity.

Joseph Norris

May 13

Happiness comes to those who are fair to others and are always just and good.

Psalm 106:3 TLB

August 20

Hearts never lose touch; friendships linger forever in a place that no words could ever describe.

May 14

A friend is a precious possession
Whose value increases with the years.
Someone who doesn't forsake us
when a difficult moment appears.
Henry Van Dyke

August 19

The real secret of happiness is not what you give or what you receive; it's what you share.

May 15

God's fingers can touch nothing but
to mold it into loveliness.
George MacDonald

August 18

Happiness is a perfume you cannot pour on others
without getting a few drops on yourself.
Ralph Waldo Emerson

May 16

The language of friendship is not words but meaning.
Henry David Thoreau

August 17

You will go out in joy and be led forth in peace; the mountains and hills will burst into song before you, and all the trees of the field will clap their hands.

Isaiah 55:12 NIV

May 17

Your friends are God's gift to you,
just as you are His gift to them.

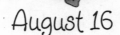

August 16

God's heart is the most sensitive and tender of all.
No act goes unnoticed, no matter
how insignificant or small.
Richard J. Foster

May 18

Encourage each other to build each other up.

1 Thessalonians 5:11 TLB

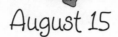

August 15

Some people make the world
special just by being in it.

May 19

Friendship is a gift from God
that's blessed in every part...
born through love and loyalty...
conceived within the heart.

August 14

Friendships begun in this world can be taken up again
in heaven, never to be broken off.
Francis De Sales

May 20

When you give of yourself,
you receive more than you give.

Antoine de Saint-Exupéry

August 13

All that we have and are is one of the unique and never-to-be-repeated ways God has chosen to express Himself in space and time. Each of us, made in His image and likeness, is yet another promise He has made to the universe that He will continue to love it and care for it.

Brennan Manning

May 21

There's a miracle called friendship
that dwells within the heart,
and you don't know how it happens
or how it gets its start...
but the happiness it brings you
always gives a special lift,
and you realize that friendship
is God's most precious gift.

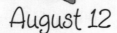

August 12

Love...keeps no record of wrongs.

1 Corinthians 13:4,5 NIV

May 22

Seeing how God works in nature can help us
understand how He works in our lives.
Janette Oke

August 11

A dream is a wish your heart makes.
Walt Disney

May 23

Every good and perfect gift is from above, coming
down from the Father of the heavenly lights,
who does not change like shifting shadows.

James 1:17 NIV

August 10

Friendship is based upon
What we give, not what we take,
And it steers its kindly course
For a special friend's own sake.

Edith H. Shank

May 24

We don't need soft skies to make friendship a joy to us.
What a heavenly thing it is;
World without end....
Such friends God has given me.

Celia Laighton Thaxter

August 9

The goodness of God is infinitely more wonderful
than we will ever be able to comprehend.
A. W. Tozer

May 25

Living the truth in your heart without compromise
brings kindness into the world.
18th Century Monk

August 8

Normal day, let me be aware of the treasure you are.
Let me learn from you, love you, bless you before you
depart. Let me not pass you by in quest of some
rare and perfect tomorrow.

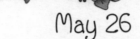

May 26

Though love be deeper, friendship is more wide.

Corinne Robinson

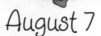

August 7

Two are better than one.... For if they fall,
one will lift up the other.
Ecclesiastes 4:9-11 NRSV

May 27

Meeting someone for the first time
is like going on a treasure hunt.
What wonderful worlds we can find in others!

Edward E. Ford

August 6

My friend is not perfect—no more than I am—
and so we suit each other admirably.
Alexander Smith

May 28

"For I know the plans I have for you," declares the Lord, "plans to prosper you and not to harm you, plans to give you hope and a future."

Jeremiah 29:11 NIV

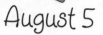

August 5

We have not made ourselves; we are the gift
of the living God to one another.

Reine Duell Bethany

May 29

A true friend is somebody who can
make us do what we can.
Ralph Waldo Emerson

August 4

It is God to whom and with whom we travel,
and while He is the End of our journey,
He is also at every stopping place.

Elisabeth Elliot

May 30

Real generosity is doing something nice for
someone who'll never find it out.

Frank A. Clark

August 3

If I were to make a solemn speech in praise of you, in gratitude, in deep affection, you would turn an alarming shade of crimson and try to escape.
So I won't. Take it all as said.

Marion Garretty

May 31

Some of the most rewarding and beautiful moments of a friendship happen in the unforeseen open spaces between planned activities. It is important that you allow these spaces to exist.

Christine Leefeldt

August 2

Embrace this God-life. Really embrace it, and nothing will be too much for you.... That's why I urge you to pray for absolutely everything, ranging from small to large. Include everything as you embrace this God-life, and you'll get God's everything.

Mark 11:22-24 MSG

June 1

Before God made us, He loved us....
And in this love our life is everlasting.
Julian of Norwich

August 1

The glory of friendship is found in the inspiration that comes when I discover that someone else believes in me and is willing to trust me with their friendship.

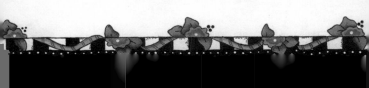

June 2

Beloved, since God loved us so much,
we also ought to love one another.

1 John 4:11 NRSV

July 31

Love in the heart wasn't put there to stay; love isn't love 'til you give it away.

Oscar Hammerstein II

June 3

My friend shall forever be my friend,
and reflect a ray of God to me.

Henry David Thoreau

July 30

Friends should be treasured. And to have good friends, you must be a good friend.

June 4

Joys come from simple and natural things:
mists over meadows, sunlight on leaves,
the path of the moon over the water.
Sigurd F. Olson

July 29

I'd like to be the sort of friend that you have been to me. I'd like to be the help that you've been always glad to be; I'd like to mean as much to you each minute of the day. As you have meant, old friend of mine, to me along the way.

Edgar A. Guest

June 5

Some people come into our lives and quickly go.
Some stay for a while and leave footprints on
our hearts and we are never, ever the same.

July 28

The Lord your God is with you.... He will take
great delight in you, He will quiet you with his love,
He will rejoice over you with singing.

Zephaniah 3:17 NIV

June 6

"Just living is not enough," said the butterfly.
"One must have sunshine, freedom, and a little flower."
Hans Christian Andersen

July 27

Hold fast your dreams!
Within you heart
Keep one still, secret spot
Where dreams may go
And, sheltered so,
May thrive and grow.

Louise Driscoll

June 7

Be kind to one another, tenderhearted, forgiving one
another, as God in Christ has forgiven you.

Ephesians 4:32 NRSV

July 26

Those who sow courtesy reap friendship, and those who plant kindness gather love.

June 8

Friendship is not diminished by distance or time...
by suffering or silence. It is in these things that it roots
most deeply. It is from these things that it flowers.

July 25

Love has its source in God,
for love is the very essence of His being.

Kay Arthur

June 9

Most new discoveries are suddenly-
seen things that were always there.
Susanne K. Langer

July 24

The first blush of friendship is a grace to behold:
a moment of shyness, a tentative hello. Every
other gift in life takes wing from here—affection,
generosity, sharing—until soon your life is rich.

June 10

Live for today but hold your hands open to tomorrow.
Anticipate the future and its changes with joy.
There is a seed of God's love in every event,
every circumstance, every unpleasant situation
in which you may find yourself.
Barbara Johnson

July 23

When others are happy, be happy with them.
If they are sad, share their sorrow.
Romans 12:15 TLB

June 11

This new day brings Another year,
Renewing hope...
Dispelling care.
And may we find
Before the end,
A deep content...
Another friend.

Arch Ward

July 22

Everyone was meant to share
God's all-abiding love and care;
He saw that we would need to know
a way to let these feelings show....
So God made hugs.

Jill Wolf

June 12

Listen to your life. See it for the fathomless mystery that it is. In the boredom and pain of it no less than in the excitement and gladness: touch, taste, smell your way to the holy and hidden heart of it because in the last analysis all moments are key moments and life itself is grace.

Frederich Buechner

July 21

Love is not getting, but giving.... It is goodness and honor and peace and pure living—yes, love is that and it is the best thing in the world and the thing that lives the longest.

Henry Van Dyke

June 13

The Lord will guide you always; He will satisfy your needs.... You will be like a well-watered garden, like a spring whose waters never fail.

Isaiah 58:11 NIV

July 20

Something deep in all of us yearns for God's beauty,
and we can find it no matter where we are.

Sue Monk Kidd

June 14

God loves and cares for us, even to the least
event and smallest need of life.
Henry Edward Manning

July 19

Friendship, like the immortality of the soul, is too good to be believed. When friendships are real, they are not glass threads or frost work, but the solidest things we know.

Ralph Waldo Emerson

June 15

Bless God for the love of friends so true,
A love akin to His,
Which knows our faults and loves us still;
That's what real friendship is.

Pat Lassen

July 18

God is love. Whoever lives in love lives
in God, and God in him.

1 John 4:16 NIV

June 16

We have been in God's thought from all eternity, and in
His creative love, His attention never leaves us.
Michael Quoist

July 17

Just as there comes a warm sunbeam into every
cottage window, so comes a love—born of
God's care for every separate need.

Nathaniel Hawthorne

June 17

There is no duty we so much underrate as the duty
of being happy. By being happy we sow
anonymous benefits upon the world.

Robert Louis Stevenson

July 16

Through the eyes of our friends, we learn to see ourselves...through the love of our friends, we learn to love ourselves...through the caring of our friends, we learn what it means to be ourselves completely.

June 18

As far as God is concerned, there is a sweet, wholesome fragrance in our lives. It is the fragrance of Christ within us.

2 Corinthians 2:15 TLB

July 15

If you can learn to laugh in spite of the circumstances that surround you, you will enrich others, enrich yourself, and more than that, you will last!

Barbara Johnson

June 19

One cannot collect all the beautiful shells on the beach.
One can collect only a few, and they are more
beautiful if they are few.

Anne Morrow Lindbergh

July 14

Friends that hold each other accountable usually have a deep, abiding, and open relationship....
Being aware that a friend cares enough to make us accountable creates a stronger bond.

June 20

Our Creator would never have made such lovely days, and given us the deep hearts to enjoy them, above and beyond all thought, unless we were meant to be immortal.

Nathaniel Hawthorne

July 13

Say only what is good and helpful to those you are talking to, and what will give them a blessing.

Ephesians 4:29 TLB

June 21

From quiet homes and first beginning
Out to the undiscovered ends.
There's nothing worth the wear of winning,
But laughter and the love of friends.

Hilaire Belloc

July 12

Every act of kindness bears the signature of love.

Janet Weaver Smith

June 22

A best friend is like a completion—
they make you better than you are.

July 11

Line by line, moment by moment, special times are
etched into our memories in the permanent ink of
everlasting love in our relationships.

Gloria Gaither

June 23

May the God of hope fill you with all joy
and peace as you trust in him.

Romans 15:13 NIV

July 10

A kind heart is a fountain of gladness, making everything in its vicinity freshen into smiles.
Washington Irving

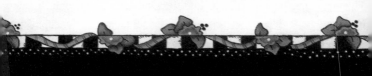

June 24

What made us friends in the long ago
When we first met?
Well, I think I know;
The best in me and the best in you
Hailed each other because they knew
That always and always since life began
Our being friends was part of God's plan.

George Webster Douglas

July 9

We do not understand the intricate pattern of the stars in their courses, but we know that He who created them does, and that just as surely as He guides them, He is charting a safe course for us.

Billy Graham

June 25

Every good thing multiplies when it is shared
by two with the same heart.

July 8

Let God have all your worries and cares, for he is always thinking about you and watching everything that concerns you.

1 Peter 5:7 TLB

June 26

Teach us delight in simple things.
Rudyard Kipling

July 7

There is nothing better than the encouragement
of a good friend.

Katherine Butler Hathaway

June 27

Having someone who understands is a great blessing
for ourselves. Being someone who understands
is a great blessing to others.

Janette Oke

July 6

God makes our lives a medley of joy and tears,
hope and help, love and encouragement.

June 28

If we walk in the light, as he is in the light,
we have fellowship with one another.
1 John 1:7 NIV

July 5

To discover a kindred spirit is to find your
heart in the heart of a friend.
Ann D. Parrish

June 29

Life is what we are alive to. It is not length but breadth.... Be alive to...goodness, kindness, purity, love, history, poetry, music, flowers, stars, God, and eternal hope.

Maltbie D. Babcock

July 4

The ordinary acts we practice every day at home are of more importance to the soul than their simplicity might suggest.

Sir Thomas More

June 30

The miracles of nature do not seem miracles because they are so common. If no one had ever seen a flower, even a dandelion would be the most startling event in the world.

July 3

For God is sheer beauty, all generous in love,
loyal always and ever.
Psalm 100:5 MSG

July 1

How beautiful a day can be when
kindness touches it.
George Elliston

July 2

Where your pleasure is, there is your treasure:
where your treasure, there your heart;
where your heart, there your happiness.

Augustine